START-UP
HISTORY

THE GREAT FIRE OF LONDON

Stewart Ross

Evans Brothers Limited

Published by Evans Brothers Limited
2A Portman Mansions
Chiltern Street
London W1U 6NR

Reprinted 2003, 2005, 2006, 2007, 2008

Produced for Evans Brothers Limited by
White-Thomson Publishing Ltd.
Bridgewater Business Centre,
210 High Street, Lewes, East Sussex BN7 1UP

Printed in China by WKT Co. Ltd

Editor: Anna Lee
Consultant: Norah Granger
Designer: Tessa Barwick
Map Illustration: The Map Studio

Cover (centre): a painting of the Great Fire of London
  by Lieve Verschuier.
Cover (top left): seventeenth century firefighters.
Cover (top right): pages of Samuel Pepy's diary.

British Library Cataloguing in Publication Data

Ross, Stewart
  Great Fire. - (Start-up history)
  1.Great Fire, London, England, 1666 - Juvenile literature
  2.London (England) - History - 17th century -
  Juvenile literature
  I.Title
  942.1'066

ISBN 978 0 237 52411 1

Picture Acknowledgements: Bridgeman Art Library/
Gavin Graham Gallery 5; Bridgeman Art Library/Museum
of London 7 (bottom); Bridgeman Art Library/
Corporation of London 19; Bridgeman Art Library/
O'Shea Gallery, London 18-19; Bridgeman Art Library/
Private Collection (cover, centre), (title page), 4, 4-5, 18
(top); Bridgeman Art Library/Royal Society of Arts 8 (top);
Bridgeman Art Library/Simon Carter Gallery 7 (top);
Mary Evans Picture Library 10, 11; Museum of London
16-17; Pepys Library, Magdalene College, Cambridge
(cover, top right), 8 (bottom); Piers Cavendish/Impact 13;
The National Portrait Gallery 9; Topham Picturepoint 12,
15; Topham Picturepoint/London Fire Brigade Museum
(cover, top left), 14.

VISIT OUR WEBSITE
www.evansbooks.co.uk
Evans

Contents

The Great Fire of London

▶ A very long time ago,
London looked like this.

The old city of London was
burned in a great fire.
This happened almost
350 years ago.

4

▲ These people watched
the flames from boats
on the River Thames.

After the fire, the city
was rebuilt.

▲ This Monument was built
so that people remember
the Great Fire.
It is still standing today.

flames   river   rebuilt   today   5

When was the Great Fire of London?

These numbers are years.

We also call them dates.

What is the date today?

100 years is called a century.
In the timeline each century
is a different colour.

The Great Fire of London
was in the year 1666.

— 1666

1600

1700

1800

1900

2000

2100

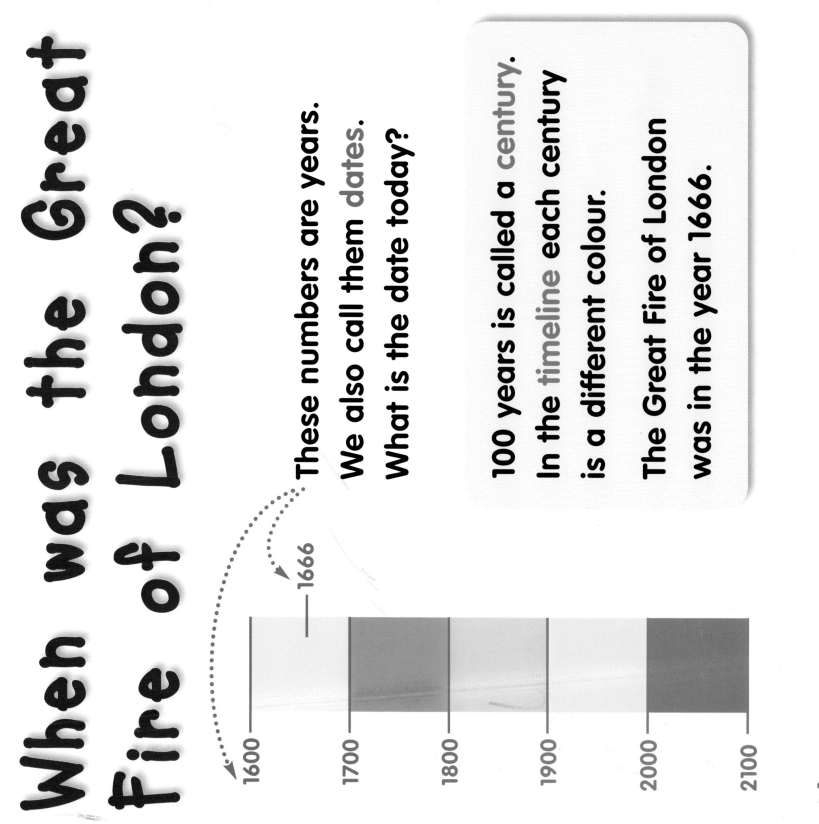

dates   century

6

▲ This is King Charles II.
He was the King
of England in 1666.

▼ Here is a painting of the fire.
Is it night-time or daytime?
Paintings like this tell us
about the fire.

How do we know about the Great Fire?

▲ This is Samuel Pepys. He lived in London at the time of the Great Fire. He wrote about the fire in his diary.

"It made me weep to see it. The churches, houses, and all on fire and flaming at once, and a horrid noise the flames made."

churches

diary

This is John Evelyn. He also wrote about the fire in his diary.

"By night it was light as day for ten miles round about."

People who watch an event are called 'eyewitnesses'. Samuel Pepys and John Evelyn were eyewitnesses to the Great Fire.

How did the Great Fire start?

The Great Fire began with a little fire in a bakery.

The bakery was in a street called Pudding Lane.

In this picture of a bakery from the past, the fire is for the oven.

began   bakery   past

The houses of old London were very close to each other.

How did the fire spread from the bakery to other houses?

oven   spread

Why did a little fire become the Great Fire?

These houses are from the time of the Great Fire.

They are built with wooden frames. We call them timber-framed.

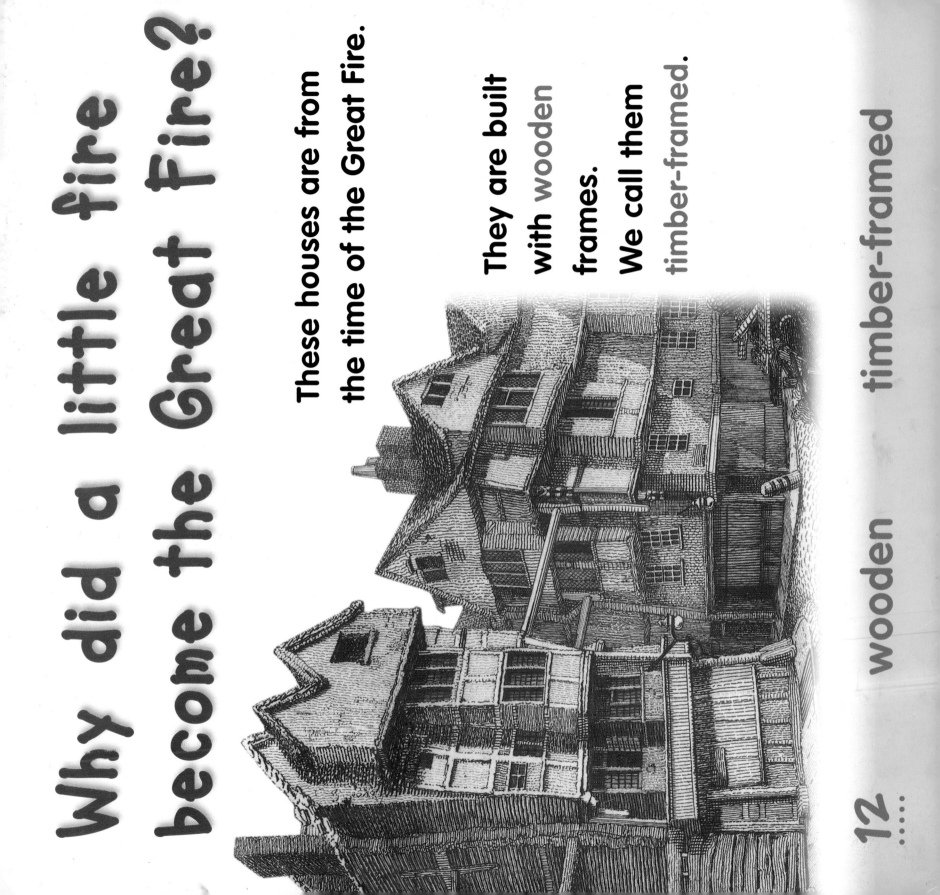

wooden   timber-framed

These are more modern houses. They are made of bricks and plaster.

Which burns best, brick or wood?

In the Great Fire the wind sent the flames from one house to another.

Pepys thought the fire would reach his house.

He moved out.

modern   bricks   plaster   wind   13

Trying to put out the fire

There was no fire brigade at the time of the Great Fire.

People had to carry water from the River Thames in buckets. It took a long time. They could not put out the big fire.

fire brigade   buckets

▲ Modern fire-fighters have fire engines to carry their hoses and ladders. They can stop a fire spreading to other houses.

After the Great Fire

The Great Fire of London lasted for five days. It burned 13,200 houses.

Cathedral of S. Paul

THE RIVE

The top picture shows what London looked like before the fire.

lasted   before

The bottom picture shows what it looked like afterwards.

Many people had no homes.

Pepys' house was not burned down.

You can see that many churches were still standing.

Why were they not destroyed?

afterwards   homes   destroyed

Building a new city

▶ This is Christopher Wren. He planned a pleasant new London with wide streets and houses of stone and brick.

The old London was crowded and dirty. The new city was cleaner and healthier.

planned   streets   stone   crowded

► Before the fire,
St Paul's Cathedral
was the most
famous building in
all London. After the
fire, it was a ruin.

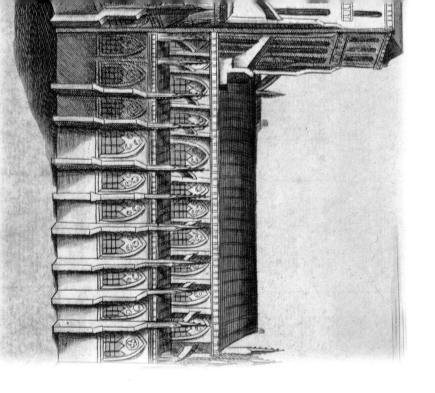

► Christopher Wren built this
new St Paul's Cathedral.
How is it different from
the old one?
It is still standing today,
but parts of it have changed.

dirty   cleaner   healthier   ruin

The story of

Here is a map of
London in 1666.
The yellow, orange
and red areas
burned down.

Use these pictures
to tell the story of
the Great Fire.

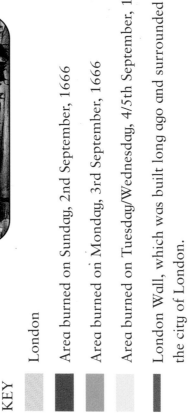

ALDERSGATE STREET

St Paul's
Cathedra

LUDGATE HILL

HOLBORN

FETTER LANE

R I V E R

KEY

London

Area burned on Sunday, 2nd September, 1666

Area burned on Monday, 3rd September, 1666

Area burned on Tuesday/Wednesday, 4/5th September, 1666

London Wall, which was built long ago and surrounded
the city of London.

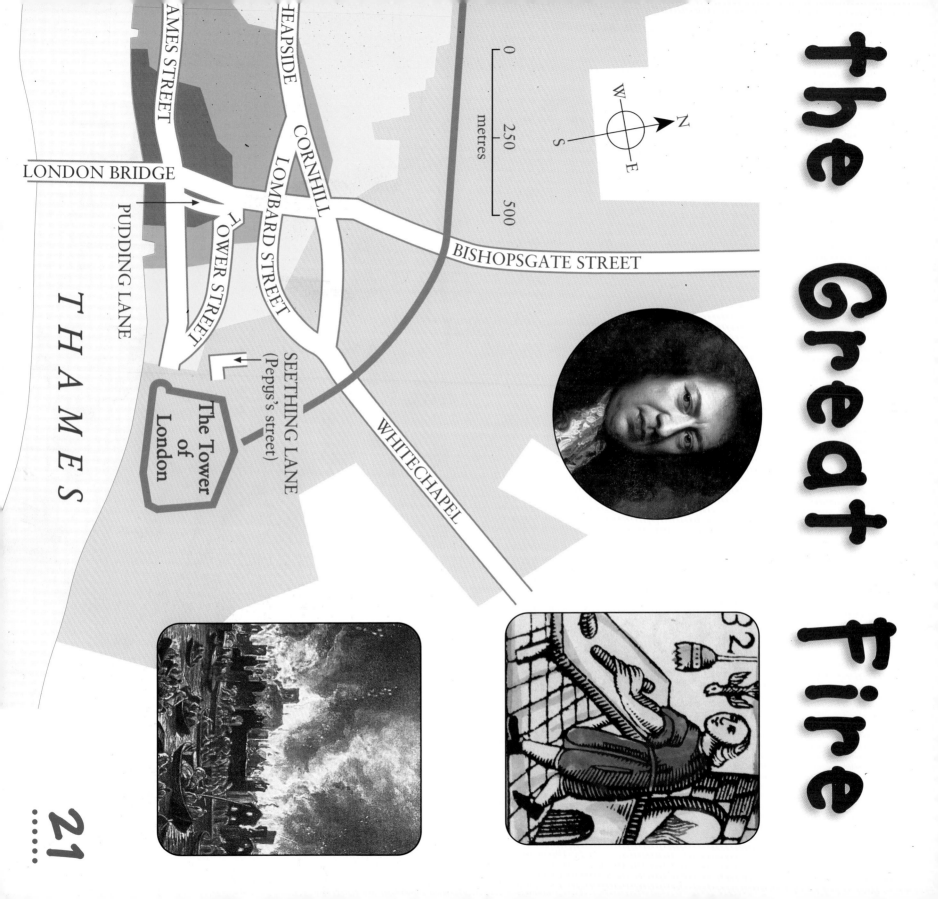

the Great Fire

THAMES STREET

CHEAPSIDE

CORNHILL

LONDON BRIDGE

LOMBARD STREET

PUDDING LANE

TOWER STREET

SEETHING LANE
(Pepys's street)

The Tower
of
London

BISHOPSGATE STREET

WHITECHAPEL

0
metres
250
500

W N S E

Further information for

New history words and words about the Fire of London listed in the text:

ago
afterwards
bakery
before
began
bricks
buckets
burned
century
churches

cleaner
crowded
dates
destroyed
diary
dirty
engines
eyewitnesses
fire
fire brigade

fire fighters
flames
healthier
homes
hoses
houses
ladders
lasted
miles
modern

old
oven
painting
past
planned
plaster
rebuilt
river
ruin
spread

stone
streets
timber-framed
timeline
today
wind
wooden
years

Background Information

THE GREAT FIRE

The fire raged from 2 to 6 September 1666, early in the reign of Charles II. It was blamed (falsely) on foreigners, especially the Dutch (with whom the country was at war) and the Catholic French. The blaze destroyed 89 churches as well as St Paul's. The fire began at a baker's in Pudding Lane and the Monument (1671-5) was erected near there. Plans for a wholly new city were rejected, but parliament did regulate to make further fires less likely (stipulating building materials, etc.). Significantly, the city was never again smitten with an outbreak of plague as virulent as that of 1665.

CHARLES II

The fire took place during the reign of Charles II (1660-1685), son of the executed Charles I. The king was at Westminster when the fire broke out. He showed some alacrity in ordering houses in the path of the flames to be pulled down or blown up. Memory of the disastrous fire, widely blamed on Catholics, fuelled the Exclusion Crisis of 1679-81, when parliament attempted to bar the king's brother, the Roman Catholic James Duke of York, from the succession.

CHRISTOPHER WREN

Sir Christopher Wren (1632-1723) became surveyor-general of the king's works in 1669. He developed a passionate interest in architecture and was the principal architect for the rebuilding of London after the fire.

SAMUEL PEPYS

A sharp-witted civil servant, Samuel Pepys (1633-1703) served as Secretary to the Admiralty from 1672-9 and 1684-88. Pepys' candid record of his life between 1660 and 1669 was written in a form of shorthand that was not deciphered until 1825. Often published, (sometimes bowdlerised), it has established itself as a popular literary classic and an invaluable and accessible source of information on Restoration England.

JOHN EVELYN

After fighting for the king during the Civil Wars (1642-48), Evelyn (1620-1706) travelled abroad. He returned with Charles II and became a familiar figure at court and a founder member of the Royal Society. A collector and patron of the arts, he wrote a number of works besides his famous diary.

ST PAUL'S CATHEDRAL

The 'Old St Paul's', burned down in the Great Fire, was begun in Norman times and completed in the fourteenth century. It was the longest building in Britain and the third longest cathedral in Europe. After the fire, the cathedral was patched up for services. However, subsequent structural collapses persuaded the authorities to start again. Work on the new building, designed by Christopher Wren, began in 1675 and was completed in 1708 – 42 years after the Great Fire.

Possible Activities:

Read selected and edited passages from Pepys diary.

Discuss the role of eyewitnesses in historical events. Write diaries.

Draw pictures of the fire.

Make a class frieze timeline.

Compare the map on pages 20-21 with a map of London today.

Some Topics for Discussion:

Which tells us more about the fire, Pepys or a painting?

Why did the fire start /stop?

The role of the River Thames (escape route / barrier, etc.).

How did London benefit from the Great Fire?

Further Information

BOOKS
FOR CHILDREN

The Great Fire of London by G. Clements (Watts, 2001)

The Great Fire of London by Jill Atkins (Hodder Wayland, 1998)

Great Plague and Fire – London in Crisis by Richard Tames, (Heinemann, 1998)

FOR ADULTS

London – the Biography by Peter Ackroyd (Chatto and Windus, 2000)

The Great Fire of London by Stephen Porter (Sutton, 2001)

The Shorter Pepys by Robert Latham (Penguin, 1993)

The Concise Pepys by Lord Braybrooke (Wordsworth, 1997)

WEBSITES

http://www.jmccall.demon.co.uk/history/page2.htm

http://www.thehistorynet.com/BritishHeritage/articles/1995_text.htm

http://www.hinchbk.cambs.sch.uk/diaries/fire.html

http://www.britainexpress.com/History/great_fire.htm

http://www.angliacampus.com/education/fire/london/history/greatfir.htm

http://www.bbc.co.uk/history/games/fire/index.shtml

http://www.schoolhistory.co.uk/year8links/greatfire.html

PLACES TO VISIT

The Museum of London

Great Fire Monument, London

St Paul's Cathedral

Any town or city with wooden houses in ancient, narrow streets.

Index